SHOW TUNES
CAR SONGBOOK

THINK BROADWAY

DAVID MERRICK'S
42ND STREET

Directed and Choreographed by
GOWER CHAMPION

SHOW TUNES
CAR SONGBOOK

Compiled by Gary Delfiner

RUNNING PRESS • PHILADELPHIA, PENNSYLVANIA

Printed in Hong Kong.

CANADIAN REPRESENTATIVES:
General Publishing Co., Ltd.
30 Lesmill Road
Don Mills, Ontario M3B 2T6.
INTERNATIONAL REPRESENTATIVES:
Worldwide Media Services, Inc.
115 East 23rd Street
New York, NY 10010.

ISBN 0–89471-605-0 (paper)
ISBN 0–89471-606-9 (library binding)
ISBN 0–89471-607-7 (package)

This book may be ordered
by mail from the publisher.
Please include $1.00 postage.
But try your bookstore first!
Running Press Book
Publishers, 125 South Twenty-second Street, Philadelphia,
Pennsylvania, 19103.

Cover design by Toby Schmidt
Cover illustration by
Tom Herbert
Photographs by
Sharon Wohlmuth
Typography: Clearface by rci,
Philadelphia; Franklin Gothic
Condensed by Letraset
Printed by South Sea
International, Ltd., Hong Kong

CONTENTS

Dedicated to Coco Margolis,
whose support and guidance
helped me get my show on the road.

NOTE TO SINGERS

The songs in this book were written to help tell
a story, and many of them were introduced by a
few lines that were spoken or sung. We've in-
cluded those introductory lines to preserve the
feeling of those original songs and to add to
your enjoyment.

ACKNOWLEDGMENTS

Andy Hopkins, my "Show Tune Source"
    Thanks, Andy!
Joan Perri of A.S.C.A.P.
Jay Morganstern of Warner Bros. Publications
Peter Wright of Chappel/Intersong
Joseph Weiss of Eastman & Eastman Publishing
Arthur Valando of Thomas Valando Publishing
Lester Boles of Alley Music
Ellen and Barbara, "The Show Tune Sisters"

GIVE MY REGARDS TO BROADWAY
FROM LITTLE JOHNNY JONES

Did you ever see two Yankees part
up on a foreign shore
When the good ship's just about
to start for old New York once
more?
With tear-dimmed eye, they say
goodbye, they're friends
without a doubt.
When the man on the pier shouts,
"Let them clear," as the ship
strikes out.

Say hello to dear old Coney Isle, if
there you chance to be
When you're at the Waldorf, have
a smile and
charge it up to me.
Mention my name ev'ry place you
go, as 'round the town you
roam
Wish you'd call on my gal, now
remember, old pal, when you
get back home.

7

Give my regards to Broadway
Remember me to Herald Square
Tell all the gang at Forty-second
    Street that I will soon be there.

Whisper of how I'm yearning
To mingle with the old time throng
Give my regards to old Broadway
    and say that I'll be there e'er
    long.

Give my regards to Broadway
Remember me to Herald Square
Tell all the gang at Forty-second
    Street that I will soon be there.

Whisper of how I'm yearning
To mingle with the old time throng
Give my regards to old Broadway
    and say that I'll be there e'er
    long.

9

GET ME TO THE CHURCH ON TIME
FROM MY FAIR LADY

I'm getting married in the morning
  Ding! dong! the bells are gonna
    chime
Pull out the stopper
Let's have a whopper
But get me to the church on time!

I gotta be there in the morning
Spruced up and looking in my
    prime
Girls, come and kiss me
Show how you'll miss me
But get me to the church on time!

If I'm dancing, roll up the floor!

If I am whistling, whewt me out the
    door!

For I'm getting married in the
    morning
Ding! dong! the bells are gonna
    chime
Kick up a rumpus
But don't lose the compass
And get me to the church
Get me to the church
For Pete's sake, get me to the
    church on time

(Repeat)

11

SOME ENCHANTED EVENING
FROM SOUTH PACIFIC

Some enchanted evening
You may see a stranger
You may see a stranger across a
crowded room

And somehow you know
You know even then
That somewhere you'll see her
again and again

Some enchanted evening
Someone may be laughing

You may hear her laughing across a
crowded room

And night after night, as strange as
it seems
The sound of her laughter will sing
in your dreams
Who can explain it? Who can tell
you why?
Fools give you reasons, wise men
never try

Some enchanted evening

When you find your true love
When you feel her call you across a
crowded room
Then fly to her side and make her
your own

Or all through your life you may
dream all alone

Once you have found her, never let
her go.
Once you have found her, never let
her go!

13

CLOUDY
COOLER

LINDY'S

PALACE

PALACE

PALACE

PALACE

La Cage
aux

La Cage
aux

14

GETTING TO KNOW YOU

FROM THE KING AND I

It's a very ancient saying
  But a true and honest thought
That if you become a teacher
By your pupils you'll be taught.
As a teacher, I've been learning
      (you'll forgive me if I boast)
And I've now become an expert on
      the subject I like most
Getting to know you.

Getting to know you, getting to
      know all about you
Getting to like you, getting to hope
      you like me

Getting to know you, putting it my
      way, but nicely
You are precisely my cup of tea!

Getting to know you, getting to feel
      free and easy
When I am with you, getting to
      know what to say.
Haven't you noticed? Suddenly I'm
      bright and breezy
Because of all the beautiful and new
Things I'm learning about you
Day by day.

Getting to know you, getting to
    know all about you
Getting to like you, getting to hope
    you like me
Getting to know you, putting it my
    way, but nicely
You are precisely my cup of tea!

Getting to know you, getting to feel
    free and easy
When I am with you, getting to
    know what to say.
Haven't you noticed? Suddenly I'm
    bright and breezy
Because of all the beautiful and new
Things I'm learning about you
Day by day.

HELLO, DOLLY!
FROM HELLO, DOLLY!

I went away from the lights of
    Fourteenth Street
  And into my personal haze
But now that I'm back in the lights
    of Fourteenth Street
Tomorrow will be brighter than the
    good old days!

Hello, Dolly, well hello, Dolly
It's so nice to have you back where
    you belong
You're looking swell, Dolly, we can
    tell, Dolly
You're still glowin', you're still
    crowin', you're still goin' strong.

We feel the room swayin', for the
    band's playin'
One of your old fav'rite songs from
    'way back when,
So
Take her wrap, fellas,
Find her an empty lap, fellas,
Dolly'll never go away again!

Hello, Dolly, well hello, Dolly
It's so nice to have you back where
    you belong
You're looking swell, Dolly, we can
    tell, Dolly

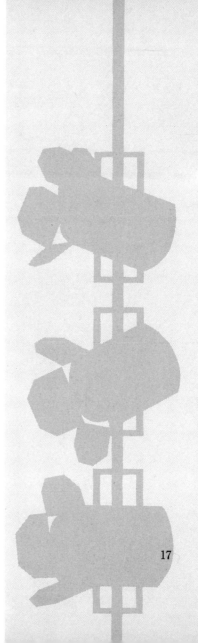

You're still glowin', you're still
    crowin', you're still goin'
    strong.

We feel the room swayin', for the
    band's playin'
One of your old fav'rite songs from
    'way back when,
So
Golly gee, fellas,
Find her a vacant knee, fellas,
Dolly'll never go away,
Dolly'll never go away,
Dolly'll never go away again!

19

TOMORROW
FROM ANNIE

The sun'll come out tomorrow
Bet your bottom dollar that
tomorrow there'll be sun!
Jus' thinking about tomorrow
Clears away the cobwebs and the
sorrow till there's none

When I'm stuck with a day that's
gray and lonely
I just stick out my chin and grin and
say:
Oh! the sun'll come out tomorrow

So you got to hang on til tomorrow
come what may!
Tomorrow, tomorrow, I love ya,
tomorrow
You're always a day away

The sun'll come out tomorrow
Bet your bottom dollar that
tomorrow there'll be sun!
Jus' thinking about tomorrow
Clears away the cobwebs and the
sorrow till there's none

When I'm stuck with a day that's
gray and lonely
I just stick out my chin and grin and
say:
Oh! the sun'll come out tomorrow
Oh! I got to hang on till tomorrow
come what may!
Tomorrow, tomorrow, I love ya,
tomorrow, you're always a
day away!
Tomorrow, tomorrow, I love ya,
tomorrow, you're only a day away!

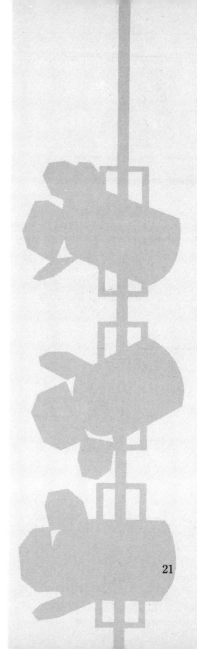

IF I LOVED YOU
FROM CAROUSEL

When I worked in the mill
Weavin' at the loom
I'd gaze absent-minded at the roof
And half the time the shuttle'd
   tangle in the threads
And the warp'd get mixed with the
   woof
If I loved you!
Oh, somehow I can see just exackly
   how I'd be

Kinda scrawny and pale
Pickin' at my food
And love-sick like any other guy
I'd throw away my sweater and

dress up like a dude
In a dickey and a collar and a tie
If I loved you!
And I know I would be like you said
   you'd be with me

If I loved you, time and again I
   would try to say
All I'd want you to know.

If I loved you, words wouldn't come
   in an easy way,
'Round in circles I'd go
Longin' to tell you, but afraid and
   shy

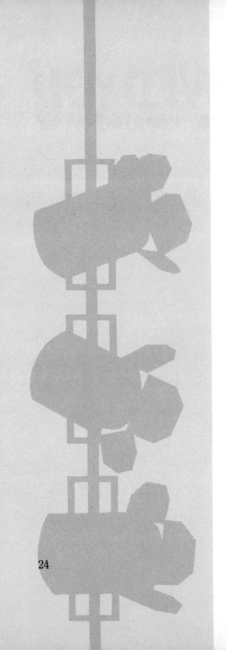

*I'd let my golden chances pass me
    by!
Soon you'd leave me, off you would
    go in the mist of day
Never, never to know
How I loved you
If I loved you*

*If I loved you, time and again I
    would try to say
All I'd want you to know.*

*If I loved you, words wouldn't come
    in an easy way,
'Round in circles I'd go
Longin' to tell you, but afraid and
    shy
I'd let my golden chances pass me by!
Soon you'd leave me, off you would
    go in the mist of day
Never, never to know
How I loved you
If I loved you*

IF I WERE A RICH MAN

FROM FIDDLER ON THE ROOF

If I were a rich man
 Daidle, deedle, daidle, digguh,
   digguh, deedle, daidle, dum
All day long I'd biddy, biddy bum
If I were a wealthy man.

Wouldn't have to work hard
Daidle, deedle, daidle, digguh,
   digguh, deedle, daidle, dum
If I were a biddy, biddy rich
Digguh, digguh, deedle daidle man.

I'd build a big tall house with rooms
   by the dozen, right in the
   middle of the town

A fine tin roof with real wooden
   floors below
There could be one long staircase
   just going up and one even
   longer coming down
And one more leading nowhere just
   for show.

I'd fill my yard with chicks and
   turkeys and geese and ducks
   for the town to see and hear
Squawking just as noisily as they can
And each loud quack and cluck and
   gobble and honk will land like
   a trumpet on the ear

25

As if to say here lives a wealthy
 man.

If I were a rich man
Daidle, deedle, daidle, digguh,
 digguh, deedle, daidle, dum
All day long I'd biddy, biddy bum
If I were a wealthy man.

Wouldn't have to work hard
Daidle, deedle, daidle, digguh,
 digguh, deedle, daidle, dum
If I were a biddy, biddy rich
Digguh, digguh, deedle daidle man.

I see my wife, my Golde, looking
 like a rich man's wife, with a
 proper double chin
Supervising meals to her heart's
 delight
I see her putting on airs and
 strutting like a peacock, Oy!
 What a happy mood she's in
Screaming at the servants day and
 night.

The most important men in town
 will come to fawn on me
They will ask me to advise them
Like Solomon the wise

*"If you please, Reb Tevye, pardon
     me, Reb Tevye."*
*Posing problems that would cross a
     rabbi's eyes.*
*Boi, boi, boi, boi, boi, boi, boi,
     boi, boi*
*And it won't make one bit of
     diff'rence if I answer right or
     wrong*
*When you're rich, they think you
     really know.*

If I were rich, I'd have the time that
*I lack, to sit in the synagogue
     and pray*
*And maybe have a seat by the
     eastern wall*
*And I'd discuss the holy books with
     the learned men seven hours
     ev'ry day*
*This would be the sweetest thing of
     all.*

If I were a rich man
*Daidle, deedle, daidle, digguh,
     digguh, deedle, daidle, dum*

All day long I'd biddy, biddy bum
If I were a wealthy man.

Wouldn't have to work hard
Daidle, deedle, daidle, digguh,
  digguh, deedle, daidle, dum
Lord, who made the lion and the
  lamb
You decreed I should be what I am
Would it spoil some vast eternal
  plan
If I were a wealthy man?

29

SEND IN THE CLOWNS
FROM A LITTLE NIGHT MUSIC

Isn't it rich?
 Are we a pair?
Me here at last on the ground, you
 in mid-air
Send in the clowns.

Isn't it bliss?
Don't you approve?
One who keeps tearing around, one
 who can't move
Where are the clowns?
Send in the clowns.

Just when I'd stopped
Opening doors

Finally knowing the one that I
 wanted was yours
Making my entrance again with my
 usual flair
Sure of my lines
No one is there.

Don't you love farce?
My fault, I fear.
I thought that you'd want what I
 want. Sorry, my dear
But where are the clowns?
Quick, send in the clowns.
Don't bother, they're here.

Isn't it rich?
Isn't it queer?
Losing my timing this late in my
      career?
And where are the clowns?
There ought to be clowns.
Well, maybe next year.

OKLAHOMA
FROM OKLAHOMA!

Brand new state! Brand new state,
Gonna treat you great!

Gonna give you barley, carrots and
    pertaters
Pasture for the cattle, spinach and
    termayters!
Flowers on the prairie where the
    June bugs zoom
Plen'y of air and plen'y of room.
Plen'y of room to swing a rope!
Plen'y of heart and plen'y of hope.

*Oklahoma, where the wind comes
    sweepin' down the plain*

*And the wavin' wheat can sure
    smell sweet
When the wind comes right behind
    the rain*

*Oklahoma, every night my honey
    lamb and I
Sit alone and talk
And watch a hawk
Makin' lazy circles in the sky*

*We know we belong to the land
And the land we belong to is grand!
And when we say Yeeow!
A yip-i-o-ee ay!*

33

We're only sayin'
You're doin' fine, Oklahoma!
Oklahoma O.K.

Oklahoma, where the wind comes
    sweepin' down the plain
And the wavin' wheat can sure
    smell sweet
When the wind comes right behind
    the rain

Oklahoma, every night my honey

lamb and I
Sit alone and talk
And watch a hawk
Makin' lazy circles in the sky

We know we belong to the land
And the land we belong to is grand!
And when we say Yeeow!
A yip-i-o-ee ay!
We're only sayin'
You're doin' fine, Oklahoma!
Oklahoma O.K.

TRY TO REMEMBER
FROM THE FANTASTICKS

Try to remember the kind of
  September when life was slow
  and oh, so mellow
Try to remember the kind of
  September when grass was
  green and grain was yellow
Try to remember the kind of
  September when you were a
  tender and callow fellow
Try to remember and if you
  remember, then follow

(Echo)
Follow, follow, follow, follow, follow,
  follow, follow, follow

Try to remember when life was so
  tender that no one wept
  except the willow
Try to remember when life was so
  tender that dreams were kept
  beside your pillow
Try to remember when life was so
  tender that love was an ember
  about to billow
Try to remember and if you
  remember, then follow

(Echo)
Follow, follow, follow, follow, follow,
  follow, follow, follow

36

Deep in December it's nice to
remember altho' you know the
snow will follow
Deep in December it's nice to
remember without a hurt the
heart is hollow
Deep in December it's nice to
remember the fire of
September that made us mellow
Deep in December our hearts should
remember and follow

(Echo)
Follow, follow, follow, follow, follow,
follow, follow, follow, follow

37

38

WHAT I DID FOR LOVE
FROM A CHORUS LINE

Kiss today goodbye
The sweetness and the
    sorrow
We did what we had to do
And I can't regret what I did for
    love
What I did for love

Look, my eyes are dry
The gift was ours to borrow
It's as if we always knew
But I won't forget what I did for
    love

What I did for love

Gone, love is never gone
As we travel on
Love's what we'll remember

Kiss today goodbye
And point me toward tomorrow
Wish me luck, the same to you
Won't forget, can't regret what I did
    for love
What I did for love
What I did for love

39

SEVENTY-SIX TROMBONES
FROM THE MUSIC MAN

Seventy-six trombones led the big
    parade
With a hundred and ten cornets
    close at hand
They were followed by rows and
    rows of the finest virtuosos,
    the cream of ev'ry famous
    band

Seventy-six trombones caught the
    morning sun
With a hundred and ten cornets
    right behind
There were more than a thousand
    reeds springing up like weeds

There were horns of ev'ry shape
    and kind

There were copper bottom tympani
    in horse platoons
Thundering, thundering, all along
    the way
Double bell euphoniums and big
    bassoons
Each bassoon having his big fat say

There were fifty mounted cannon in
    the battery
Thundering, thundering, louder than
    before

41

Clarinets of ev'ry size and
    trumpeters who'd improvise
A full octave higher than the score

Seventy-six trombones led the big
    parade
When the order to march rang out
    loud and clear
Starting off with a big bang bong on
    a Chinese gong
By a big bang bonger at the rear

Seventy-six trombones hit the
    counterpoint
While a hundred and ten cornets
    played the air
Then I modestly took my place as
    the one and only bass
And I oom-pahed up and down the
    square

Seventy-six trombones hit the
    counterpoint
While a hundred and ten cornets
    played the air
Then I modestly took my place as
    the one and only bass
And I oom-pahed, oom-pahed, oom-
    pah-pahed, oom-pahed up and
    down the square

LULLABY OF BROADWAY
FROM 42ND STREET

Come on along and listen to
   The lullaby of Broadway
The hip hooray and ballyhoo
The lullaby of Broadway

The rumble of the subway train
The rattle of the taxis
The daffydils who entertain
at Angelo's and Maxie's

When a Broadway baby says
    "Good night"
It's early in the morning
Manhattan babies don't sleep tight
Until the dawn:

Good night, baby, good night
Milkman's on his way
Sleep tight, baby, sleep tight
Let's call it a day
Hey!

Come on along and listen to
The lullaby of Broadway
The hi-dee-hi and boop-a-doo
The lullaby of Broadway

The band begins to go to town
And everyone goes crazy
You rock-a-bye your baby 'round
'til everything gets hazy

43

*"Hush-a-bye, I'll buy you this and
      that"*
You hear a daddy saying
And baby goes home to her flat
To sleep all day:

Good night, baby, good night
Milkman's on his way
Sleep tight, baby, sleep tight
Let's call it a day

*Listen to the lullaby of old
      Broadway.*

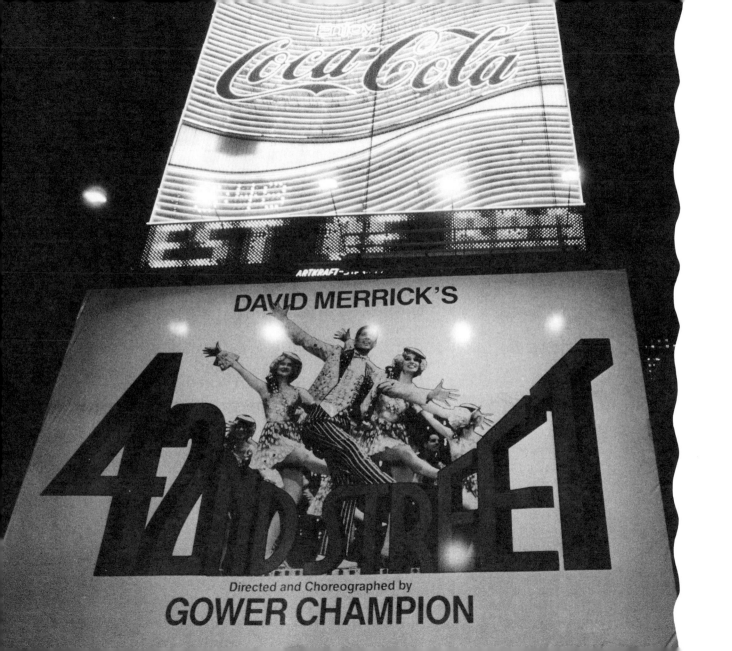

SUMMERTIME
FROM PORGY AND BESS

Summertime an' the livin' is
   easy,
Fish are jumpin', and the cotton
   is high
Oh, yo' daddy's rich, an' yo' ma is
   good lookin'
So hush, little baby, don' you cry

One of these mornin's you goin' to
   rise up singin'
Then you'll spread yo' wings an'
   you'll take the sky
But till that mornin', there's a-nothin'
   can harm you
With Daddy an' Mammy standin' by

CLIMB EV'RY MOUNTAIN
FROM THE SOUND OF MUSIC

Climb ev'ry mountain
Search high and low
Follow ev'ry by-way, ev'ry path you
*   know.*

Climb ev'ry mountain
Ford ev'ry stream
Follow ev'ry rainbow till you find
*   your dream!*

A dream that will need
All the love you can give
Ev'ry day of your life
For as long as you live.

Climb ev'ry mountain
Ford ev'ry stream
Follow ev'ry rainbow till you find
*   your dream!*

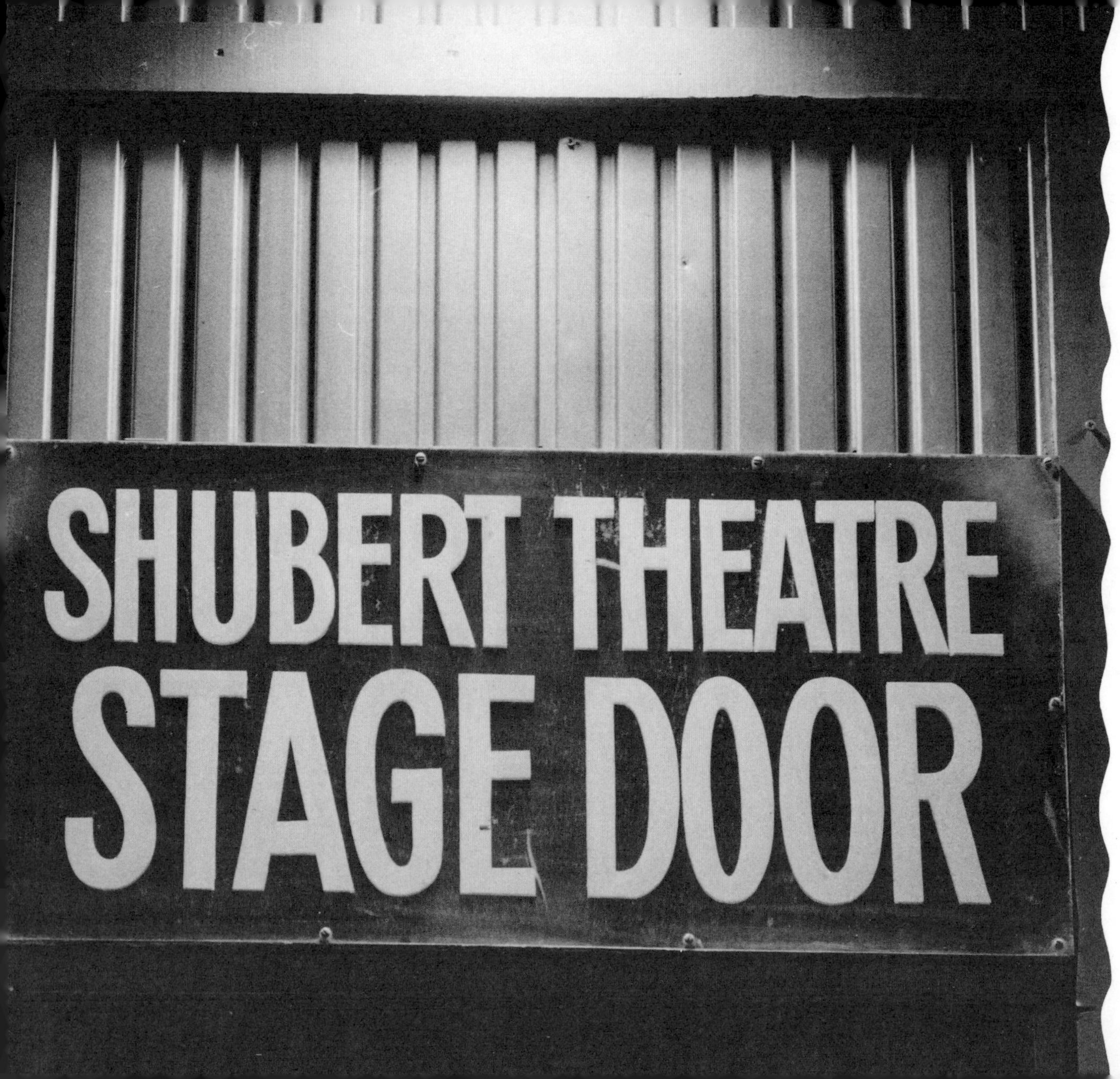
SHUBERT THEATRE
STAGE DOOR